AMAZING SCIENCE
SOUND

Sally Hewitt

WAYLAND

Published in paperback in 2014 by Wayland
Copyright © 2014 Wayland

Hachette Children's Books
338 Euston Road, London NW1 3BH

Senior Editor: Joyce Bentley
Senior Design Manager: Rosamund Saunders
Designer: Tall Tree

British Library Cataloguing in Publication Data
Hewitt, Sally
      Sound. - (Amazing Science)
      1. Sound - Juvenile literature
      I. Title
      534

ISBN-13: 978-0-7502-8061-7

Printed and bound in China

10 9 8 7 6 5 4 3 2 1

Wayland is a division of Hachette Children's Books, an Hachette UK Company.
www.hachette.co.uk

Cover: A grizzly bear on its hind legs, growling
Title page: Boy playing drum kit in his bedroom

NASA/Corbis 6, Jon Hicks/Corbis 7, Stone/Getty Images 8, Mel Yates/Getty Images 9,
Photorgapher's Choice/Getty Images 10, Stone/Getty Images 11, Reportage/Getty images
12, Frank Blackburn/Ecoscene 13, Stone/Getty Images 14, David Tipling/Getty Images 15,
David Pu'u/Corbis 16, Bruno Levy/zefa/Corbis 17, Stone/Getty Images 18, Frans
Lanting/Corbis 19, Royalty-Free/Corbis 20, Karl-Heinz Haenel/zefa/Corbis 21, Joe
McDonald/Getty images 22, Robert Essel NYC/Corbis 23, Stone/Getty images 24,
Stone/Getty Images 25, The Image Bank/Getty Images 26, Stone/Getty images 27,

Contents

Amazing sound

The moon is quiet and still. There is no air to make sounds and no wind to blow the footprints in the dust.

Sound is made by moving air, so without air, there is no sound.

Our planet Earth is surrounded by air. It is a noisy, busy place.

YOUR TURN!

Listen. What can you hear? Do you know what is making the sound?

Traffic, rain on umbrellas and people talking are all sounds we hear.

SCIENCE WORDS: **air quiet sound**

Vibrations

A humming bird beats its wings so fast they look like a blur. The wings move the air and we hear a hum.

We hear sounds when moving air goes into our ears.

When you hit a drum the air around it vibrates, or moves very fast. This makes the sound.

YOUR TURN!

Put your hand on the TV while it is on. Can you feel the vibrations?

When we bang a drum the vibrating air goes into our ears as a sound.

SCIENCE WORDS: **hear   vibrations**

Ears

A herd of elephants walk through the savannah. Their enormous ears listen out for danger.

Ears are shaped so they can pick up sounds.

We hear with our ears. Two ears help us to hear sounds all around us.

YOUR TURN!

Cup your hand round your ear to make it bigger. Can you hear better now?

We hear our friends talking with our ears.

SCIENCE WORDS: ears shaped

Loud and quiet

Loud sounds can damage your ears. An aircraft handler protects his ears from the sound of the jet aircraft.

The ear drum and tiny bones inside your ears vibrate when sound goes into your ears.

Quiet sounds are made by small vibrations in the air and loud sounds are made by large vibrations.

YOUR TURN!

Clap loudly. Clap quietly. What do you do to make a loud and quiet clap?

A mouse makes a quiet sound.

SCIENCE WORDS: loud quiet

Low and high

A bear's low growl rumbles through the forest. It scatters deer and can scare the birds out of the trees.

People and animals make sounds with the voice box in their throat.

High sounds are made by fast vibrations. Low sounds are made by slow vibrations.

YOUR TURN!

Gently feel the voice box in your throat while you make low and high sounds. What happens to it?

A small bird makes a high sound when it sings.

SCIENCE WORDS: high   low   voice box

Big and small

Enormous waves roll onto a beach. They break onto the sand with a loud crashing sound.

When the waves are big, the sea makes a loud sound.

When the waves are small, the sea makes a quiet sound. You have to listen carefully to hear it.

YOUR TURN!

Why do you think a still pool of water makes no sound at all?

When the sea is calm and quiet, it only moves a little.

SCIENCE WORDS: move still

Travelling sound

In a thunderstorm, flashes of lightning split the sky. A few seconds later, thunder crashes with a loud bang.

Light travels faster than sound so you see the lightning flash before you hear the bang of thunder.

Sound needs something to travel through. It travels through air, water, the ground and even walls.

YOUR TURN!

Listen. What have the sounds you hear travelled through to reach your ears?

The sound of whales singing to each other travels through water.

SCIENCE WORDS: **listen   through   travel**

19

Near and far

A truck rumbles along the highway. Its engine sounds louder and louder as it gets closer and closer.

The nearer you are to a noise, the louder it sounds.

Sound becomes quieter as it travels through the air. A noise coming from far away sounds quiet.

As the plane goes up in the sky it gets quieter.

SCIENCE WORDS: far near

Echoes

Bats dart through the night sky catching insects to eat. They use their ears to find insects in the dark.

The sound of the squeak hits an insect and bounces back into the bat's ears as an echo.

The bat then knows where the insect is to catch it.

When you shout in a cave, your voice bounces off the walls and you hear an echo.

YOUR TURN!

Bounce a ball off a wall to see how an echo works. Your voice bounces back off the wall, just like a ball.

SCIENCE WORDS: bounce echo

Music

Musicians in an orchestra blow, bang, pluck and shake instruments to make sounds. These sounds make music.

Tubes of air, strings and drum skins vibrate when instruments are played.

Short strings play higher notes and longer strings play lower notes.

YOUR TURN!

Make instruments. Put rice, beans or pasta into containers with lids. Shake them and hear the different sounds.

A cello player presses the strings to make them shorter.

Sending sound

Your voice can travel to a satellite in space and back to earth again. You can talk to someone far away.

The sound of your voice is sent through space on invisible radio waves.

Many phones are attached to a wire called a land line.

Your voice travels from phone to phone along the wires.

YOUR TURN!

Do you think a mobile phone sends sounds along wires or radio waves?

SCIENCE WORDS: **radio waves   satellite   wires**

Glossary

Air
An invisible gas all around us.

Bounce
To hit something and jump back off it quickly.

Ears
The part of your body that you hear with.

Echo
You hear an echo when the sound of your voice bounces off something and back into your ears.

Far
When something is far, it is a long way away.

Hear
You hear when sounds go into your ears.

High
A sound that is the opposite of deep. A bird singing is a high sound.

Instruments
Something you blow, bang, pluck or shake to make a musical sound.

Listen
To pay attention to hearing sounds.

Loud
A sound that is strong and easy to hear. A road drill and thunder make loud sounds.

Low
A sound that is deep. A bear growling and a big drum make low sounds.

Move
Something is moving when it is not still.

Near
Something is near when it is close to you.

Notes
Notes are musical sounds made by singing or by a musical instrument.

Quiet
A little noise or no noise at all.

Radio waves
Invisible waves in the air that carry sound.

Satellite
An object that goes round Earth in space and sends messages back from space.

Shaped
Everything has a shape. Ears are shaped so that they can pick up sounds easily.

Sound
A noise that is made when the air vibrates.

Still
When things are not moving, they are still.

Through
When you go through something, you pass through the middle of it.

Travel
To go from one place to another.

Vibrations
To make tiny, very fast movements.

Voice box
The part of your body that makes sounds when you speak.

Wire
A long string made of metal.

Index